Guess Who's Coming Out At Dinner?

Guess Who's Coming Out At Dinner?

Julian Lake

Guess Who's Coming Out At Dinner?

Published in the United States by Rubicon Media, P.O. Box 1823, Radio City Station, New York, New York 10101-1823

First Rubicon Media Edition: February 1999

10 9 8 7 6 5 4 3 2 1

PRINTED IN THE UNITED STATES OF AMERICA.

Library of Congress Catalog Card Number: 98-68356

ISBN: 0-9663454-1-X

For everyone who has ever
been there and done that.

"Thanks for coming out on Christmas, son.
Your mother and I really can't think of
a better present."

"Dear, don't you think there are enough
lesbians in America already?"

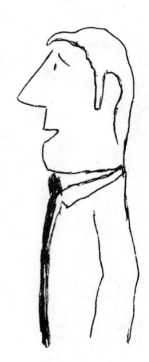

"Rumor has it that I'm gay."

"Just how gay are you?"

"Now, mom and dad, when you remove the paper bags there will be a gay person standing in front of you."

"I just can't believe that you are gay. You were such a sweet little boy when you were growing up."

"You're a lesbian? Don't you think we should get a second opinion?"

"Why did you have to come out to us now?
Couldn't you have waited until we
were dead?"

"You just think you're gay because everyone
on television is."

"You really don't have to wear those. No one's
gonna recognize that you're parents
of a gay."

"Yes, mother, I'm gay in the Biblical sense
of the word."

"Your father and I are not going to see your
name in some big lesbian Who's Who,
are we?"

"Mom, I'm heterosexual, but I've decided to adopt the gay lifestyle."

"Dad, I do everything you do in bed, but backwards and in high heels."

"Dear, just promise me one thing. No ugly girlfriends."

"Between glee club and cheerleading, we kind of knew it was all over."

"Carol, this is my son, the gay."

"Young lady, you're grounded until you're
not a lesbian any more."

"Dear, maybe you're confusing lesbianism with millennial Angst."

"Well, I see you went right out and bought
the uniform."

"Okay, lay it on us son. You're gay as
a goose, aren't you?"

"We'll get through this, dear. Let's all just take it one lesbian day at a time."

"Oh, it's National Coming Out Day? That's very thoughtful of you to remind us. Now, son, what did you want to talk to us about?"

"Don't take it so personally, son. Your mother always cries at coming outs."

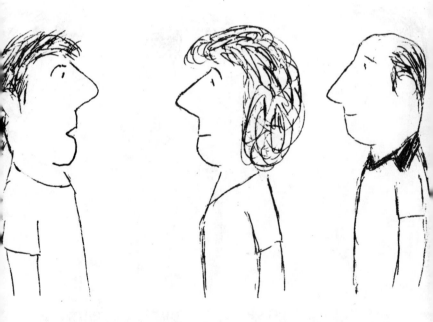

"Now I'd like to teach you and father the secret gay and lesbian handshake."

"I thought I'd go gay for a couple of years and then, if things don't work out, I'll settle down, get married, and raise a family."

"When I was young we didn't have
sexual orientations."

"Mother, I'm gay. It's a guy thing."

"I hate men too, dear, but I'm not a lesbian."

"Thank you for leaving the message that you're gay on our answering machine. Your mother's been playing it for the neighbors all day."

"Your father was just saying this morning that he
hoped you would tell us that you're a lesbian
so we can spend our retirement years
at women's softball games."

"Fasten our seatbelts because it's going to be
a bumpy night? Son, what's that
supposed to mean?"

"Now that you're a lesbian, will you be needing less money for clothes?"

"How can you be gay? You don't have any
disposable income."

"Mother, in order to succeed in the theater, I've
decided to become a homosexual."

So everyone on your field hockey team turned
out to to be a lesbian? Isn't that
a coincidence!"

"Vell, father, it turns out that I'm not an insufferable name-dropping, pretentious little prig after all. I'm gay!"

"Mother, it would help me feel more accepted if you didn't constantly refer to me as Little Miss Lesbian Smarty-pants."

"Is your lover gay too, dear?"

"Young lady, I hope coming out doesn't mean
lesbian pajama parties till all hours
of the morning."

"Son, now that you've come out, your mother
wants you to move to New York City and
find out which of her favorite soap
opera stars is gay."

"Just because you've slept with two hundred
women doesn't mean that you're a lesbian."

"A queen? Of what country?"

"Well, you did turn out to be a man's man."

"You woundn't be a lesbian if you had come
with me to Jenny Craig."

"My girlfriend Shirley is so lucky. Her children
never came out to her."

"No, not Albanian mother. . . lesbian!"

"Couldn't you just get married and have a
stud or two on the side?"

"Mother, today is the first day of
the rest of my gay life."

"Well, Candace, maybe there's a little bit of
lesbian in all of us."

"Let's put it this way, mother. I'm not even
on the Kinsey scale."

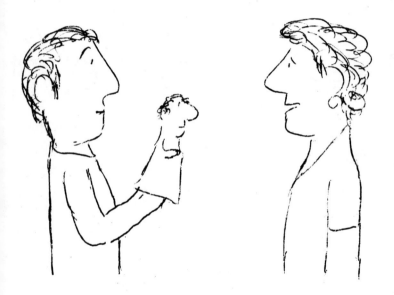

"Oh, you're just trying to break it to me gently.
Your handpuppet's not gay. You are!"

"But dear, your mother and I can't really afford
a big lesbian wedding."

"Now that you know I'm gay, I'd like you to meet my insignificant other."

"Of course you're a lesbian. You couldn't think of any better way to hurt your mother."

"Son before you decide that you're gay, I want you to try Viagra."

"Of course the first thing your father's sister said was that she always thought my side of the family was loaded with lesbians."

"Your father and I didn't have a clue that
you were gay, Miss Thing."

"Well dear, even for a lipstick lesbian, I think that's a bit too much lipstick."

"What do you mean you're gay? This isn't the Sixties, you know."

"Let's just say that my biological clock is now ticking in the lesbian time zone."

"Mother, I'd like you to meet my soul mate,
Mr. Leather of 1994."

"I don't care if you're a lesbian. You're buying
a turkey baster and you're giving
me grandchildren."

"Your father and I want our own float in the
Gay Pride parade."

"Edmund, old boy, you're not gay. You're British."

"And son, will you be getting gayer?"

"Son, I don't want to be cut out of your life just because you're gay. Can I be your fag hag?"

"Be honest. What upsets you more? That I'm
a lesbian or that I'm a Martian."

"And is it true that the mothers of gays tend
to be more attractive than the
mothers of nongays?"

"Mother, what can I tell you? Sometimes the
right woman turns out to be a drag queen."

"Son, you may be gay, but you'll still always be mommy's poopsie-woopsie-uggams-wuggams."

"So Tammy, how long have you known that you
are a you-know-what."

"Son, I think I liked you better as a closet queen."

"Now, why on earth are you changing your
name to Sappho?"

"But son, except for the tiara, you certainly
don't look gay."

"No, Grandmother. Even if I had eaten more of your Christmas mincemeat pies as a child, I still would have become a lesbian."

"You're gay because we couldn't afford to send you to Yale, aren't you?"

"Very funny, Sarah. When I was a girl I used to kid around and tell my mother I was a lesbian too!"

"And which one of you guys does the nagging?"

"I think you've got it all wrong. You were probably
a lesbian in a past life."

"Mother, I'm gay and this is your granddaughter, Fifi."

"Son, tell your mother that you're gay again.
I love it when she screams like that."

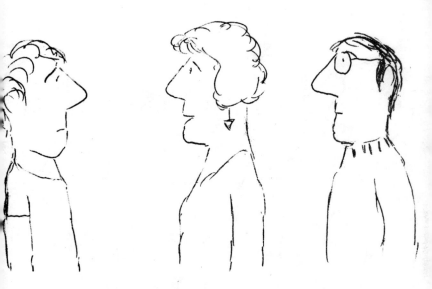

"Your father thinks that you're gay because
he never watched Jeopardy with you."

"Why don't you two just have a good buddy
ceremony and leave it at that?"

"Son, if you're so goddamned gay, why do you let your mother go out looking the way she does?"

"Just promise me one thing, son. That you'll never turn your life into a gay cartoon."

About the Author

Julian Lake was a member of the famous Lake family which was considered to be the century's greatest trapeze circus acts until Julian came out to his father during a performance. After his father's funeral, Julian devoted his life to helping people come out safely to their parents. He has lectured on coming out all over the world. Thanks to Julian Lake, coming out is no longer a high-wire act for millions of gay men and lesbians. This is his first cartoon book.

About the Publisher

Rubicon Media is a company founded in 1998 to publish bestselling fiction, nonfiction and humor for a gay, nongay and kind-of-gay audience. Our mission is to publish works that combine fine literary taste with crass commercialism.

This is Rubicon Media's second book. Our first was a novel called *Iron Peter* by Charles Ortleb. In *Continuum*, Celia Farber compared the satirical novel to *Animal Farm* and said "it may be the most dangerous book of the decade."